FOUR DIMENSIONS
OF HUMAN HEALTH

PERSONAL DEVELOPMENT EXPERIENCE

LOVEAND**TRANSFORMATION** INSTITUTE

Four Dimensions of Human Health
Personal Development Experience
Ben Bost and Kent DelHousaye © 2019
Love and Transformation Institute

Four Dimensions logo courtesy of Eli Bost.

All Bible references from New Living Translation (NLT) unless otherwise specified.

Print ISBN: 978-1-73398-7-905
eBook ISBN: 978-1-73398-7-912

For more information, visit LoveandTransformation.org

Published by

Love and Transformation Institute

Printed in the United States of America

TABLE OF CONTENTS

PREFACE +

How will you grow?

Our guess is that your interest in the Four Dimensions of Human Health comes from your desire to be a different person.

However, growth doesn't necessarily mean you'll be different. Consider a tree—as it grows it simply becomes a bigger and more fruitful version of itself. It does not become something entirely new.

The Four Dimensions of Human Health is designed to help you establish a philosophy of maturity that takes into account the beauty of who you already are and who you are becoming.

In it you will:

- Discover the four areas of holistic development
- Become aware of surrounding issues that impact growth in each area
- Learn how to integrate love into all dimensions of life.

The sessions inside are segmented into four areas each designed to help you grow, providing a balanced and well-rounded approach. As you move through the experience it is important to remember that each session holds unique value to its given dimension and the overall experience.

The Four Dimensions of Human Health can be used in the following ways:

- Individual study
- One-on-one mentoring
- Small group study
- Large gatherings

For more information about how to use this experience in your unique setting, do not hesitate to contact us at info@loveandtransformation.org.

Love Well!

Ben Bost
Kent DelHousaye
Co-Founders
Love and Transformation Institute

✚ INTRODUCTION

"The function of education is to teach one to think intensively and to think critically. But education which stops with efficiency may prove the greatest menace to society. The most dangerous criminal may be the man gifted with reason but no morals . . . We must remember that intelligence is not enough. Intelligence plus character—that is the goal of true education."

–Martin Luther King Jr., speech at Morehouse College, 1948

THE VALUE OF LEARNING

The ability to learn is an incredible privilege and powerful opportunity!

And learning is not designed just to shape your mind through acquiring knowledge. It is also meant to shape you as an individual while that knowledge is put into action. For a learning process to be most effective, it must be multidimensional. When this well-rounded approach is utilized, it naturally forms people into mature and responsible human beings who can contribute to society and the well-being of our world!

Jesus said, "A student is not above his teacher, but everyone when he is fully trained will be like his teacher" (Luke 6:40).

At the Love and Transformation Institute, we believe that to be "fully trained" means experiencing holistic development in what we call the *Four Dimensions of Human Health*—emotional, relational, intellectual, and vocational.

These Four Dimensions are drawn directly from Jesus when he affirmed the greatest life is found when you *"Love the Lord your God with all your heart, all your soul, all your mind, and all your strength"* (Mark 12:30).

THE ROLE OF LOVE

We believe growth is not about becoming a different person. Instead, it is the process of becoming aware of who you already are and learning to love well as that person. This is our philosophy of maturity.

Love becomes the driving factor of your personal growth.

God has designed each of us in His image with unique qualities and characteristics meant to reflect who He is to the world around us, His primary character quality being love (1 John 4:18).

But each of us has encountered brokenness in life that has, in essence, stunted our growth and affected our ability to love well. The first step to kickstarting our growth is learning what love is and how it functions.

Mostly, we approach love as an emotion. However, it is much more than a romantic sentiment, flood of passion, or thought expressed. And this is where we must begin.

We must think about love differently!

Love is active and structural, providing architecture to all of life. That is because love cannot be forced—it is chosen. And choosing love as the primary influence of your growth is what will help you integrate it into all of life. This understanding of love is key to your development.

THE PROCESS OF CHARACTER STRUCTURING

Character structuring is the process that helps you develop durability for living all of life. Throughout this experience, you will learn how the structuring of your character is influenced by each dimension and impacted by the associated topics. Each topic is designed for interaction and discussion and will assist you in developing a philosophy of maturity based on the model of the Four Dimensions of Human Health below.

EMOTIONAL

HEART – Emotional Processing

Loving God with your heart means you are learning and growing in how to have a healthy emotional life.

RELATIONAL

SOUL – Relational Processing

Loving God with your soul means you are learning and growing in how to have healthy relationships.

MIND – Intellectual Processing

Loving God with your mind means you are learning and growing in knowledge, how to think well about life.

STRENGTH – Using your Influence

Loving God with your strength means you are learning and growing in how to put your unique design into action.

INTELLECTUAL

VOCATIONAL

HEART
Emotional

Loving God with your heart means you are learning and growing in how to have a healthy emotional life. This section provides you with exercises and information to help you process your emotions and create a healthier emotional life.

EMOTIONAL

HEART – Emotional Processing

Loving God with your heart means you are learning and growing in how to have a healthy emotional life.

RELATIONAL

SOUL – Relational Processing

Loving God with your soul means you are learning and growing in how to have healthy relationships.

MIND – Intellectual Processing

Loving God with your mind means you are learning and growing in knowledge, how to think well about life.

INTELLECTUAL

STRENGTH – Using Your Influence

Loving God with your strength means you are learning and growing in how to put your unique design into action.

VOCATIONAL

WHAT IS CHARACTER?

Character is defined as the mental or moral qualities distinctive to an individual.

Other character-related words include these: personality, nature, temperament, disposition, mentality, and makeup.

You may think character is what guides you to do the right thing or tell the truth. However, character is much more substantial than that.

It is the qualities shaped in us that help us live all of life.

WHY IS CHARACTER IMPORTANT?

"Character is the set of capacities needed to meet the demands of reality."

–Dr. John Townsend

Often we don't understand we lack character in a certain area until it is tested by a challenge, stress, or great difficulty.

Character functions in your life the way steel beams function in a skyscraper. The beams provide structural integrity to keep the building from collapsing when pressure is applied. Without testing, you *can't know* if your character is durable or fragile. The outcome of character structuring is the development of a stable internal character–structure–that can "meet the demands of reality."

 **PROCESS** – How would you like your character to grow or change?

HOW DO YOU STRENGTHEN YOUR CHARACTER?

Strengthening your character begins first by understanding character structure, or the internal architecture needed to withstand the pressures, expectations, and requirements of life. According to Jesus in the sermon on the mount, healing and growth occurs from the *inside* out (Matthew 5-7).

Your internal character structure is made up of four parts that work together to create a strong foundation. *Growth occurs by understanding and expanding your capacity in each of the following areas:*

- Building connected relationships
- Setting limits with yourself and others
- Navigating both positive and negative realities
- Managing the responsibilities of life

 **PROCESS** – Which area above most resonates with you as an opportunity to strengthen your character?

CHARACTER

1.1

WHAT IS FAMILY?

Rudyard Kipling defined family as "All of us are we—and everyone else is they." (Us/Them)

Typically, *family* refers to biological family—or your *Family of Origin (FOO).*

Naturally, you look to your family for guidance as you grow into adulthood. But the family is also designed to perform three core functions:

- Provide for your physical and emotional well-being
- Protect you from harm
- Train you for life

A healthy family will perform these core functions, taking into account that all members need two essential elements to drive development: *discipline and instruction*.

Ephesians 6:4 says, "Parents, do not provoke your children to anger, but bring them up in the discipline and instruction of the Lord."

Proper discipline provides the necessary correctional training for behavior. Instruction is the formative learning about life. Unfortunately, not every home functions in a healthy or optimum way all of the time. When your home life is unhealthy or less than optimal, it can impact the structuring of your character.

UNDERSTANDING THE IMPACT OF YOUR FAMILY

Understanding how your character has been impacted by your FOO is not always easy. For some, traumatic encounters with realities such as divorce, anger, abuse, or control were normalized in the home. Others may have experienced a peacefully functioning home that lacked an explanation of life. Regardless of the circumstances, you can end up feeling confused about how you were raised and sensing you didn't get all you needed for living life.

The first step in understanding the impact of your FOO is awareness.

 **PROCESS** – In the space below, write a short description of what it was like to grow up in your family home. Describe both positive and negative experiences along with what you wish happened more/less.

NOT ALL FAMILY IS FOO

Part of developing awareness is recognizing that not all family is FOO.

We all have people in our lives who can contribute to our ongoing process of character structuring in a healthy way. This presents us with the opportunity to develop character structuring capacity through *building connected relationships.* These are the kinds of relationships that provide you space to process life.

 **PROCESS** – List a minimum of one but no more than three people in your life who you believe can be a connected relationship. Then set up a time to share with them the description of your FOO from above and invite feedback.

WHAT IS NEGATIVE REALITY?

When you were growing up, how did your parents deal with your anxiety, sadness, and anger?

If you are like most, your parents usually told you to "go to your room and change your attitude." The question is why? Why did your parents send you away when you were anxious, sad, or angry?

This response is also why we may hide our drama from others and avoid theirs. Many of us were raised to believe that emotions like anxiety, sadness, and anger are bad. But being sad, mad, anxious, and exhausted is part of the human experience.

In our culture, it's no longer acceptable to have a bad day. We've become so obsessed with happiness that experiencing normal, difficult emotions is out of line and cause for questioning one's mental health.

Negative reality is the other side of life, not fun and easy. It is hard and painful.

UNDERSTANDING NEGATIVE REALITY

God created human beings to be like Him creatively, rationally, relationally, and *emotionally!* (Genesis 1:26-27)

We read in Scripture that God Himself gets angry and sad (Deuteronomy 9:20; 1 Kings 11:9; Genesis 6:6). We get angry and sad because of negative reality. The truth is that we live in a fallen world, corrupted by sin, that is not what God made it to be. And, in a fallen world, there is suffering, pain, and loss—a lot of negative reality.

We cannot control negative reality, but we can control our *response* to it.

THE IMPORTANCE OF INTEGRATION

Learning to respond well to negative reality in your life is called *integration.*

An integrated person is able to handle negative feelings and experiences, including loss, imperfection, failure, and rejection. That is because **integration is the ability to deal with BOTH positive AND negative realities in life.**

Integration is a key skill that assists in your character structuring. It helps you process life in an honest and authentic way.

 **PROCESS** – Describe below how you normally deal with negative reality and what the influences were that caused you to view it this way

NEGATIVE REALITY

1.3

WHAT IS VULNERABILITY?

According to the dictionary, vulnerability is the quality or state of being exposed with the possibility of being attacked or harmed, either physically or emotionally.

Sound like fun?

The thought of risking and being exposed to the point of being hurt is something we naturally avoid—especially in our relationships. But vulnerability plays a vital role in helping us see life and our relationships accurately.

Vulnerability paves the way for lasting and life-giving relationships that aid in character structuring.

THE BENEFIT OF VULNERABILITY

To appreciate the value of vulnerability, you first have to distinguish between *hurt* and *harm*.

Harm is always bad but hurt is not. Hurt can often be good and necessary to benefit your growth.

Take for example the process of fitness training. Rarely are the hours of lifting weights and aerobic exercise enjoyable. Most of the time, it hurts! But over time, the benefit dramatically outweighs the pain.

Opening up about your life exposes you to critique and feedback in a way that hurts. However, it is a necessary experience to fully understand who you are and how others experience you in relationships.

HOW TO DEVELOP VULNERABILITY

A great way to develop vulnerability is to start opening up in relationships about difficult aspects of your life. Share with individuals you have chosen wisely. The more vulnerable you become, the less exposed you will feel in that relationship.

The skill of showing vulnerability says to others, "I have nothing to hide."

 **PROCESS** – Do you know one person who demonstrates vulnerability in a valuable way? Schedule a time with them to discuss how they learned to be vulnerable and why they value it.

WHAT IS GRIEF?

"Grief is the pain that cures all other pains."

–Dr. John Townsend

Grief is the natural emotional pain we experience when we encounter loss or significant change.

These are some events that can cause grief:

- Death of a loved one
- End of a relationship
- Loss of a job
- Moving
- Change

These are just a few examples of what can cause grief. It's important to understand that grief is a normal part of life and healthy emotional functioning. Feelings of sadness and uncertainty will occur when we encounter hard and painful experiences.

WHY IS GRIEVING IMPORTANT?

Grieving is the active processing of the emotions that come with loss.

Your ability to do this well as a part of character structuring is critical to your overall emotional health and well-being. Unfortunately, in our current culture, you may have been trained to get over it quickly or even skip it altogether.

Not taking the time to grieve loss dramatically increases the potential for stress, anxiety, depression, isolation, exhaustion, insomnia, stomach and heart problems, and even death.

 **PROCESS** – How were you taught to deal with loss and grief?

A HEALTHY VIEW OF GRIEF

Jesus said, "God blesses those who mourn, for they will be comforted" (Matthew 5:4). "Blessed" was just one of the words Jesus used to communicate happiness to those who heard him teach. According to Jesus, a truly happy person possesses the ability to grieve in a healthy way.

The Apostle Paul in 2 Corinthians 7:10 says, " . . . the kind of sorrow God wants us to experience leads us away from sin and results in salvation. There's no regret for that kind of sorrow."

So, what does this tell us about grief? That it is good and for our benefit!

 **PROCESS** – Is there a past loss in your life that you never really grieved? How would it be helpful to you emotionally or physically to grieve that loss?

WHAT IS STRESS?

Dictionary definition: Mental or emotional strain or tension resulting from adverse or very demanding circumstances.

According to health experts, stress is America's number one health problem, as it is estimated that at least 75 percent of all doctor visits are for stress-related problems.

In an article published in *Prevention* magazine, three of four people self-identify as "stressed out."

Stress fundamentally is pressure or tension that is tied to change. Any change, whether it is realized or imagined, can create stress.

WHAT CREATES STRESS IN YOUR LIFE?

Below are the results of a 2017 study by the American Psychological Association (APA) to discover the common causes of stress for individuals.

- 63% – Future of our nation
- 62% – Finances
- 61% – Job
- 57% – Politics
- 51% – Crime

Other leading causes are health, relationships, media overload, and lack of sleep.

 **PROCESS** – Using the information above, what most often causes stress in your life?

SAYING "NO" INSTEAD OF "YES" TO DEAL WITH STRESS

Dealing with stress effectively means you must develop the character-structuring capacity to *set limits with yourself and others.*

Stress is often self-induced because of an inability to know "when to say when." Many people today "binge watch" a favorite show as a form of relaxation. While this may help at the beginning, the prolonged media exposure, over-stimulation, and lack of sleep has an adverse effect on stress levels.

Today you must learn to say no more than you say yes if you want to manage stress effectively. You have to be the one to set the limits. Just because someone expects you to reply to an email or text at 10 p.m. doesn't mean you have to.

PROCESS – List three key areas where you can begin saying no to help in reducing your stress.

WHAT IS ANXIETY?

"The beginning of anxiety is the end of faith, and the beginning of true faith is the end of anxiety."

–George Muller

In 1947, W. H. Auden wrote a long, six-part poem called "The Age of Anxiety" that won a Pulitzer Prize. He did not know his perspective would ring true well into our current day.

Anxiety is possibly the greatest epidemic facing our society even though we are safer, healthier, and can access information faster than at any other point in history.

BUT WHAT IS ANXIETY?

The dictionary defines anxiety as a feeling of worry, nervousness, or unease, typically about an imminent event or something with an uncertain outcome.

WHAT CAUSES WORRY AND ANXIETY IN YOUR LIFE?

Did you know that worry and anxiety are self-generated?

Though it could be triggered by external events and circumstances, it becomes abnormal or unhealthy when you obsess about the "what ifs."

A University of Florida study revealed that 40 percent of people worry about things that never end up happening, 30 percent worry about things in the past that they cannot control, 12 percent worry about their health even though they may be perfectly well, and 10 percent worry about family or friends who are fine. Only 8 percent have something real to worry about!

 **PROCESS** – Write down something that creates a great deal of anxiety for you in life. Once you identify it, think about how likely it is that this event will actually happen.

NORMAL AND ABNORMAL ANXIETY

What is the difference between a "normal" kind of anxiety and an "abnormal" one?

Normal anxiety is to have concerns or worries about finances, kids, school, work, etc. *Abnormal anxiety* is persistent, irrational, uncontrollable, debilitating worry, dread, or fixation about the future or about everything that could possibly go wrong.

The Englih word "anxiety" comes from an old English word that means "to strangle." In Mark 4:19, Jesus told us that anxieties and worries of this world "choke/suffocate" us.

So, a biblical picture of ongoing anxiety says it *strangles and fractures* us.

 **PROCESS** – With the awareness that anxiety and worry is self-generated, brainstorm some ideas about how you can shift your thinking when anxiety sets in.

WHAT IS DEPRESSION?

Have you ever thought, "I think I'm depressed"? This has become such a common conclusion today that we must wonder if we really know what depression is.

According to the APA (American Psychologists Association), depression is a mental health condition that causes persistent sadness, loss of interest, and decreased functionality at home and at work.

Depression can be mild or severe and symptoms typically include feeling sad, gaining or losing weight, sleeping too little or too much, feelings of hopelessness or worthlessness, difficulty concentrating, and thoughts of death and suicide.

WHAT CAUSES DEPRESSION?

It can be difficult to pinpoint exact causes of depression. It's often a combination of multiple factors that must all be considered. Following are factors that contribute to depression:

- Biochemistry - chemical imbalance
- Genetics - family history
- Personality - self-image, sensitivity, cynicism, selective memory
- Environmental factors - trauma, abuse, loss, illness, alcohol, drugs, stress

WHAT TO DO IF YOU THINK YOU'RE DEPRESSED

First, know that depression is a common occurrence and you're not alone.

Also, did you know the Bible contains many examples of individuals struggling with instances of overwhelming sadness and grief?

(David, Psalms 38:4-8; Elijah, 1 Kings 19:4; Jonah 4:3,9; Job 3:11,26; Moses, Exodus 32:32; Solomon, Ecclesiastes 1:18; Jeremiah 20:14,18; Jesus, Mark 14:34; Paul, Philippians 1:23)

If you suspect you're struggling with depression, we recommend you take these actions:

Ask for Help - As difficult as it may seem to reach out to another person, relationships are a tremendous benefit when dealing with depression.

Think About Your Perspective - Try to see the good in your life and practice gratitude.

Take Care of Your Body - Better sleep, diet, exercise, and avoiding drugs and alcohol can increase mood and overall well-being.

Serve - Getting outside yourself and giving to others helps you feel a part of something bigger.

Don't Rule Out Medicine and Counseling - Medical professionals can be a great help for those battling depression along with counseling or therapy to process your life history and events.

WHAT IS DESIRE?

Desire can be simply understood as setting your heart upon something.

This includes all those things you are passionate about and long for. Desire is powerful and the question is not whether you will experience desire but how and for what.

Desires are neutral—meaning they are neither good nor bad. It's how we respond to our desires that is most important in character structuring. Do our desires control us? Do we allow our desires to create unrealistic expectations for life? Being aware of these types of questions helps us to use our desires in the ways God intended.

WHAT IS HEALTHY DESIRE?

In our current day, emotion has become a significant means by which people decide whether something is good or bad, positive or negative, right or wrong. Desire is now used as a way to judge morality. You may think, "It must be good for me because I desire it," or "Because I feel bad, something must be wrong."

However, we all know that just because we want something doesn't mean it's good for us. Also, just because we are struggling doesn't mean we are not well.

This is why we must be able to separate healthy desire from unhealthy desire.

Historically, the word "lust" has often been used to characterize unhealthy desire. *Lust is being mastered by your desire in a way that controls you.*

 **PROCESS** – What are some things you have longed for in a way that mastered you in life?

HOW TO USE YOUR DESIRE

To use your desire in a healthy way, find a perspective on what you long for that comes from outside yourself.

This means you reject trusting your emotions as the primary source for understanding what is healthy and not healthy.

In the ancient world, people decided in one of three ways whether something was healthy. Was it true or real? Was it good or virtuous? Was it beautiful or excellent? Truth, goodness, and beauty can be used to evaluate what is healthy or not because they are not based on *opinion*. Something cannot be both true and not true at the same time. This also goes for goodness and beauty as well. *Something is either true, good, and beautiful or it's not.*

Learning how to use your desire in a healthy way begins by asking if what you long for is true, will result in goodness, and will produce beauty.

 **PROCESS** – What role can the Bible play in helping you understand what is true, good, and beautiful?

DESIRE

1.9

WHAT IS HAPPINESS?

"Happiness is not a destination, it's a way of life."

–Anonymous

Today, there may not be a more confusing question—especially in a culture where anxiety, depression, and suicide rates have steadily climbed for the past 75 years to an all-time high.

Answering this question is more critical than confusing, because happiness is at the core of all human existence, longing, and desire.

In the dictionary, happiness is defined as "the quality or state of being happy." But this definition doesn't help us, in practical terms, when it comes to living life.

Happiness is more than just an emotion, pleasurable high, or circumstance-based, feel-good experience. It is a strong sense of stability developed by living life a specific way. Like the quote above so clearly illustrates, happiness is found in the way we live and structure our lives.

IS HAPPINESS A GOOD GOAL?

You can't help but have happiness as the end goal for all of life. That's because you were made for it!

We've had the privilege at LTI of asking hundreds of people the question "What is the goal of life?" The answer we receive almost 100 percent of the time is "to be happy." If they don't say this, they give us a list of the things that will make them happy.

But where can we find the surest framework, paradigm, or template for cultivating a life of happiness?

Did you know the Bible has over 100 words that refer to happiness? One word used in Scripture for happiness is the word **"blessed"** and it appears over 50 times in the New Testament. Happiness is also a concept that shows up consistently throughout Scripture (Matthew 5:1-12; John 13:17, 20:29; Acts 20:35; Romans 4:7-8; 1 Timothy 1:11, 6:15; Timothy 2:13; James 1:12, 25; 1 Peter 3:14, 4:14).

Jesus even said in reference to His own mission, "The thief's purpose is to steal and kill and destroy. **My purpose is to give them a rich and satisfying life**" (John 10:10). Isn't it comforting to know God is happy and desires happiness for you as well?

 **PROCESS** – How does a biblical understanding of happiness influence your outlook on life and desire to be happy?

HOW TO PURSUE HAPPINESS

Pursuing happiness begins with a change of perspective. It's critical to understand that happiness is formed before it's felt in order to know how it will happen in your life.

As stated earlier, happiness is built over time. Character structuring helps us develop the kind of direction and stability in life that increases our well-being. Happiness comes not by seeking it directly but as a result of seeking that which produces it.

As C.S. Lewis stated in *God in the Dock*, "You cannot get second things by putting them first; you can only get second things by putting first things first." This means happiness results from living life a specific way—a way in which pleasure is not the sole focus but has its right place.

 **PROCESS** – How does the perspective above change the way you view happiness? What is the first thing you will change to begin developing a greater sense of stability?

SOUL
Relational

Loving God with your soul means you are learning and growing in how to have healthy relationships. This section will help you understand and improve your relationships with important people in your life and with God.

EMOTIONAL

HEART – Emotional Processing

Loving God with your heart means you are learning and growing in how to have a healthy emotional life.

RELATIONAL

SOUL – Relational Processing

Loving God with your soul means you are learning and growing in how to have healthy relationships.

MIND – Intellectual Processing

Loving God with your mind means you are learning and growing in knowledge, how to think well about life.

INTELLECTUAL

STRENGTH – Using Your Influence

Loving God with your strength means you are learning and growing in how to put your unique design into action.

VOCATIONAL

WHAT IS THE TRINITY?

The idea of the "Trinity" uniquely distinguishes Christianity from all other world religions.

It refers to one God existing in three persons who are all equal and distinct: God the Father, God the Son, and God the Holy Spirit.

HOW TO UNDERSTAND THE TRINITY

"Hear, O Israel: The Lord our God, the LORD is one."

–Deuteronomy 6:4

In the verse above, we see oneness emphasized in reference to God. This implies that God is unified and yet possesses multiple aspects. The ancient language of Hebrew defines the word "one" as a cluster of grapes. This illustration helps us understand the Trinity with the concept that one cluster is made up of individual grapes.

Another description of the Trinity is "tri-unity," which places the focus directly on their union!

Alister McGrath wrote that the Trinity "allows the individuality of the persons to be maintained, while insisting that each person shares in the life of the other two. An image often used to express this idea is that of a 'community of being' . . . "[1]

 **PROCESS** – How does the Trinity influence your understanding of community?

THE TRINITY AS A MODEL FOR RELATIONSHIP

Where do you find your portrait for a healthy relationship?

The picture presented of the Trinity is the epitome of relational connection. The way the three members connect and relate to one another is the primary example of how we are to relate to and connect with one another in relationship. As a soul, you are to be in connected relationship with other souls. So, it can be said that loving God with your soul means learning how to love others well.

Tim Keller described it this way: "Each of the divine persons centers upon the others. None demands that the others revolve around him. Each voluntarily circles the other two, pouring love, delight, and adoration into them. Each person of the Trinity loves, adores, defers to, and rejoices in the others. That creates a dynamic, pulsating dance of joy and love."[2]

 **PROCESS** – If you connected and related the way the members of the Trinity do, how would your relationships be different? (E.g., husband/wife, parent/child, friendship, boss/employee.)

RELATIONSHIP

2.1

THE IMPORTANCE OF FAMILY

"A family shares things like dreams, hopes, possessions, memories, smiles, frowns, and gladness . . . A family is a clan held together with the glue of love and the cement of mutual respect. A family is shelter from the storm, a friendly port when the waves of life become too wild. No person is ever alone who is a member of a family."

–Rudyard Kipling

There are two categories of families: **origin (biological)** and **choice (relational)**. Family means many things to many people, but it is essentially a household consisting of at least one parent and one or more children. Your family of origin (FOO) is your biological family, to whom you are genetically connected.

But your family of choice is your adopted family to whom you are relationally connected. When it comes to which is primary, there is a popular phrase, "blood is thicker than water." But is that true? Is your family of origin "thicker" than your family of choice?

JESUS'S PERSPECTIVE ON FAMILY

Jesus talked about becoming born again and becoming a part of the family of God. And He even suggested that becoming part of God's family is greater than your biological one.

"As Jesus was speaking to the crowd, his mother and brothers stood outside, asking to speak to him. Someone told Jesus, 'Your mother and your brothers are standing outside, and they want to speak to you.' Jesus asked, 'Who is my mother? Who are my brothers?' Then he pointed to his disciples and said, 'Look, these are my mother and brothers. Anyone who does the will of my Father in heaven is my brother and sister and mother!'"

–Matthew 12:46-50

"But to all who believed him and accepted him, he gave the right to become children of God. They are reborn–not with a physical birth resulting from human passion or plan, but a birth that comes from God."

–John 1:12-13

 **PROCESS** – How does the perspective of Jesus, described above, challenge your understanding of family? Is it encouraging? Uncomfortable?

THE FAMILY OF GOD

Because of the biological family breakdown in culture, many people struggle with a sense of belonging and not knowing who they really are or where they ultimately belong. The family of God is where we can understand who we truly are and find our place of belonging forever.

2 Corinthians 6:16,18 says, "I will live in them and walk among them. I will be their God, and they will be my people . . . And I will be your Father, and you will be my sons and daughters, says the Lord Almighty."

PROCESS – In your own words, describe the hope and people associated with the family of God in your life.

2.2

THE BREAKDOWN OF FRIENDSHIP

Today we are more connected than we've ever been in human history, and our ability to communicate with one another through multiple channels is literally at our fingertips. In a sea of social tools designed for interaction, loneliness continues to increase at epidemic rates, to the point of a public health crisis.

David Brooks wrote, "Decades ago, people typically told pollsters they had four or five close friends, people to whom they could tell everything. Now the common answer is two or three, and the number of people with no close friends has doubled. Thirty-five percent of adults report being chronically lonely, up from 20 percent a decade ago."[3]

The reality is that we all need friends and we are not meant to do life by ourselves!

THE FOUNDATION OF FRIENDSHIP

Many say, "Love is the answer." But if love is the answer, then what is the question?

The question today revolves primarily around how love is defined. It can be so confusing that we are left without the ability to understand love at even the most basic level. In the ancient language of Greek, love had four words, each communicating a different aspect of love: erotic love, parental love, divine love, and friendship.

The love that drives friendship is the kind of love meant to define all of our relationships, especially our peer relationships. It functions as an affectionate regard between equals to form a rich mutual exchange of relationship.

Just like electricity flows from one point to another, love moves from one individual to the next. It is the current that all relationship runs upon.

PROCESS – Describe how defining love influences your perspective on friendship.

THE IMPORTANCE OF FRIENDSHIP

Building a great friendship is a tremendous risk. It requires an understanding of many of the aspects covered already by Dimension One. A person's ability to be vulnerable and communicate about things like stress, anxiety, grief, or depression is what deeply bonds friends together.

The English poet John Milton noted that aloneness was the first "not good" in creation: "Loneliness was the first thing that God's eye named not good."

"The Lord God said, 'It is not good for the man to be alone.'" –Genesis 2:18

God Himself admits that a relationship with Him only is *not enough*. Also, God's admission about needing relationship is *not just* about marriage. It's about the kind of companionship true friendship provides.

PROCESS – Who are your closest friends? What are some ways you can develop a deeper friendship?

FRIENDSHIP

2.3

SETTING LIMITS AND CHARACTER STRUCTURING

As much as we need to be connected in relationship with others, we also need to know how to set limits. Finding this balance helps us maintain healthy friendships over a long period of time and it's essential to the process of character structuring.

As your character develops, it gives you the necessary ability to have healthy relationships while also maintaining a sense of your own individuality. Setting limits helps you manage people in your life appropriately, but you also need to know how to manage the stressors of life.

HOW TO SET LIMITS

Life today requires "no" more than "yes" and it's one of the key skills you must learn to manage all of life in a healthy way.

Our connected world demands from us an immediate response. Unfortunately, sometimes those closest to us can be the source of our greatest challenge in setting limits. We have to remember that structuring character builds our internal architecture to help us withstand the pressures, expectations, and requirements of life.

Drawing lines is what helps you create limits with family, friends, and the pace of life in a world of the immediate and indulgent.

According to Drs. Henry Cloud and John Townsend, boundaries are "invisible property lines" that define for us and for others where our and their responsibility begins and ends.[4]

 **PROCESS** – Describe one limit you need to set in life or in a relationship that could begin helping you right away.

THE CHALLENGE OF SETTING LIMITS

"Before daybreak the next morning, Jesus got up and went out to an isolated place to pray. Later Simon and the others went out to find him. When they found him, they said, 'Everyone is looking for you.' But Jesus replied, 'We must go on to other towns as well, and I will preach to them, too. That is why I came.'"

–Mark 1:35-38

Setting limits will not make everyone happy. Some in your life may become greatly frustrated by your efforts to create space for healthier relationship.

Possessing the ability to disengage to re-engage at your fullest capacity benefits everyone in the long run. As shown by the passage above, Jesus modeled this ability even when others questioned or required more of him.

 **PROCESS** – When you choose to disengage, what helps fill you up to re-engage?

SETTING LIMITS

2.4

WHAT IS FORGIVENESS?

"Everyone says forgiveness is a lovely idea until they have something to forgive."

–C.S. Lewis

The dictionary simply defines the word "forgive" as "to grant pardon."

In the Bible, we see two different conditions illustrated as forgiveness. For 150 times, it is "to pardon, release, or send away" and 27 times it's "to show kindness or give grace." The first is a conditional kind of forgiveness, which means there is a condition that must first be met in order to do it. The second is unconditional, meaning no conditions are needed for forgiveness to be extended.

WHY FORGIVE?

"Make allowance for each other's faults, and forgive anyone who offends you. Remember, the Lord forgave you, so you must forgive others."

–Colossians 3:13

Let's be honest--forgiveness is hard! We all can be quick to point out when someone should apologize and ask for our forgiveness and at the same time struggle to admit the wrongs we have done. It's part of the sinful human condition we all share. Yet the Bible encourages us to regularly forgive. Why? Because it's good for our health.

According to established research, there are significant physical and mental health benefits that come with forgiveness including less anxiety, lower blood pressure, greater heart health, stronger immune system, improved self-esteem, and better relationships.[5]

Not only are we to extend forgiveness to others, we must also offer that same grace to ourselves. In order to heal and grow, we must be able to let go of the guilt and shame we carry from the past. The same research also reveals that holding onto guilt and shame negatively affects our health.

 **PROCESS** - Is there something or someone in your life you need to forgive?

HOW TO FORGIVE

Dr. Henry Cloud provides a great model for forgiveness. He recommends these steps:

1. Grieve the offense - do not minimize the hurt caused
2. Metabolize the offense - process the impact of what was done
3. Move on - leave the offense behind[6]

 **PROCESS** - Decide on a time when you will try this process with the offense you listed above.

FORGIVENESS

2.5

WHAT IS EMPATHY?

The dictionary definition of empathy is "to suffer with another," and the word sympathy literally means "to feel with someone."

The ancient Greek concept for compassion means "to be moved in one's bowels or intestines," which explains why for the Greco-Roman culture, the source of one's pity or mercy was not was not their hearts but their guts.

The reality is when you "suffer with" or "feel with" someone, you experience it in your stomach. It includes entering into someone else's pain and experiencing their hurt as they do.

WHY IS EMPATHY IMPORTANT?

According to a study published in *Scientific American,* empathy and compassion are in a steep decline in our country. The research revealed that 75 percent of 14,000 college students rated themselves less empathetic than the average student did 30 years ago.[7]

It's pretty easy for us to know what empathy is not.

In a world that is driven by performance and productivity, there is little time for pain. We have been trained that when someone goes down, we simply move on.

But this was not the way of Jesus. Matthew 9:35-36 says, "Jesus traveled through all the towns and villages of that area, teaching in the synagogues and announcing the Good News about the Kingdom. And he healed every kind of disease and illness. When he saw the crowds, he had compassion on them because they were confused and helpless, like sheep without a shepherd."

Empathy is important today simply because there is such a lack of it. When we lay down ourselves and pick up the life of another, we let others know we love them and we're not unaware of what they are going through.

 **PROCESS** – Describe a recent time when you offered empathy to a close friend or family member.

HOW TO DEVELOP EMPATHY

We can develop a greater level of empathy by entering into the suffering of others in the following ways:

1. Become more aware of what others are going through
2. Be present
3. Help the other person process their emotions
4. Validate their hurt
5. Identify with the pain they are going through

PROCESS – Is there someone currently in your life who would benefit by your empathetic response to their pain?

2.6

WHAT IS COMMUNICATION?

A primary reason people struggle in life is an inability to communicate with others.

Have you found this to be true?

A concept that has over 126 definitions, according to scholars, communication can be difficult to understand. However, researcher Bill Strom offers a clear perspective on the word when he says communication is "the process by which two or more people convey messages via diverse channels with the potential for some interference."[8]

HOW DOES COMMUNICATION TAKE PLACE?

Great communication is both an art and a science. It is the path to having our ideas received and building rapport in relationships. In the process of character structuring, communication is one of the most important skills. So we must know how it works before we can improve our ability to communicate. Following are the seven phases of communication:

1. There is a "sender" who encodes a message.
2. There is a "receiver" who decodes the message.
3. There is a "medium" that carries the message.
4. There is a "context" for receiving the message.
5. There is "noise" that interrupts the message.
6. There is "feedback" given from the "receiver."
7. There are "effects" from the message shared.

Breakdown in communication occurs when "noise" gets in the way of the message, "context" for the message is not clearly established, or the message receives no "feedback" from the one who received it. For example, if a work email accidentally ends up in junk mail, then "noise" kept it from being delivered. Also, if that same email, when delivered, does not contain a clear reason why it was sent then it lacks "context" for the one who receives it. Finally, if the receiver fails to respond--then there is no "feedback" and a breakdown occurs.

 **PROCESS** – When have you experienced a breakdown in communication from "noise," lack of "context," or no "feedback"?

HOW TO BECOME A BETTER COMMUNICATOR

Becoming a better communicator is about learning how to manage "noise," "context," and "feedback."

Do everything you can to eliminate noise that prevents your message's receipt, knowing this may not always be possible. As shown by the previous illustration, you cannot control an email accidentally being flagged as junk, but you can connect with the intended "receiver" to see if it went through. Soliciting feedback means dialoguing with others about how they are experiencing your messages and then reflecting on the feedback you receive.[9]

WHAT IS CONFLICT?

Most of us would probably say we are well acquainted with conflict because of how we avoid it!

Conflict happens when there is a collision, disagreement, opposition, or clash of two people or parties, often resulting in a fight, battle, or prolonged struggle.

Why do we avoid conflict?

Conflict is a form of "negative reality" and a regular part of the human experience. Part of integrating negative reality in our lives is to process what happens to us and around us. We process conflict the same way we process food. Just as we absorb nutrients and expel waste after eating, we also absorb the healthy and expel the toxic in our conflicts. In just about every conflict, the experience of working through the conflict and seeking a resolution is valuable. And, we can assign a positive value to each conflict by the value it adds to our character.

CONFLICT IS UNAVOIDABLE

A group of historians got together at a big conference not long ago in London to compare notes and found that in 4,000 years of recorded history, only 286 of those years were peaceful in the world. Over that time, almost 15,000 (14,351) wars have been waged and at least 8,000 peace treaties have been made *and* broken!

Perhaps that is why *The New York Times* once declared that "peace is a fable."

Facts about conflict:

1. Conflict is unavoidable
2. Conflict isn't always bad
3. Conflict is an opportunity for growth
4. Conflict can be resolved

 **PROCESS** – Describe a recent conflict you were a part of and how your character changed as a result.

DOING CONFLICT WELL

Part of the character-structuring process is learning to embrace conflict as an important asset to your personal growth and development. Through it we learn to appreciate how confrontation and conflict enhances and deepens our relationships with others. When we can get past the idea that conflict is bad and stop fearing and avoiding it, then we can begin to grow and develop beyond our ability, not only personally but also relationally!

Challenge and confrontation are actually good for us and the Bible speaks of them often.

"An open rebuke is better than hidden love! Wounds from a sincere friend are better than many kisses from an enemy" (Proverbs 27:5-6).

"As iron sharpens iron, so a friend sharpens a friend" (Proverbs 27:17).

"Better to be criticized by a wise person than to be praised by a fool" (Ecclesiastes 7:5).

According to Drs. Henry Cloud and John Townsend, we actually grow personally and relationally through confrontation.[10]

WHAT IS JUSTICE?

According to *World Vision,* "Justice is first and foremost a relational term—people living in a right relationship with God, one another, and the natural creation. From a scriptural point of view, 'justice' means loving our neighbor as we love ourselves and is rooted in the character and nature of God. As God is just and loving, so we are called to do justice and live in love."[11]

There are three different kinds of justice:

- The first is **retributive** justice and it refers to punishment for offenses.
- The second is **distributive** justice and it refers to sharing benefits and burdens.
- The third is **restorative** justice and it refers to repairing victims and offenders.

WHY JUSTICE IS IMPORTANT

Justice in all its forms is a biblical issue—the Bible contains several thousand verses about justice. In the Gospels alone, one out of 10 verses is about some form of injustice. In fact, Jesus talked more about justice and injustice than about heaven and hell, violence, and sexual immorality. Justice is, in fact, the second most prominent biblical issue after misplaced worship.

Until the 20th century, there was a strong connection between the misplaced worship of a civilization and injustice—but that connection was severed sometime during the last 100 years. John Stott called this severing "The Great Reversal" because historically, through the centuries, Christians were *always* at the forefront of justice issues.

PROCESS – How do you see the misplaced worship of our culture contributing to injustice in the lives of people? In your opinion, what things we are worshipping cause this?

WHY CARE ABOUT JUSTICE?

Simple—a person with strong character cares about others and the world around them.

Micah 6:8 says, "No, O people, the Lord has told you what is good, and this is what he requires of you: to do what is right, to love mercy, and to walk humbly with your God."

Our life on display is the reflection of God's character in us (2 Corinthians 3:17-18) and paves the way for others to see the beauty that a relationship with Jesus has to offer. Stated another way, it's His glory revealed through your life and actions. This is why justice is so important. Through being just and supporting justice, we can help people understand the "good news" that awaits them in a relationship with Jesus. But it is also how we defeat the dark world and evil that seeks to destroy the good that God has for our world.

Edmund Burke said, "The only thing necessary for the triumph of evil is for good men to do nothing."

PROCESS – Can you think of issues that disturb you in our world, where you can have an impact?

THE COMMON GOOD AND GREATEST GOOD

In our last session, we discovered that until the 20th century, there was a strong connection between misplaced worship of a culture and injustice. John Stott called this modern disconnection "The Great Reversal" because historically, Christians were always at the forefront of justice issues.

What happened? Why did Christians stop caring about justice?

In the last hundred years, some Christians started believing that misplaced worship was a "religious" issue and that injustice was a "political" one. Christians and churches then began dividing into two camps—one emphasizing the "saving of souls" and the other emphasizing "social action." The essential difference between the two camps can be summarized with the terms used by John Piper in an address to the Cape Town Congress in 2010, when he said one focuses on "present suffering" and the other on "eternal suffering."

Relieving present suffering is called "social justice" while relieving eternal suffering is "evangelism" or sharing of the "good news." Social justice is about the **common good** but evangelism is about the **greatest good**, and Thomas Aquinas wrote that "the greatest good anyone can do to his neighbor is lead him to the truth." So, on one hand, relieving eternal suffering seems more important.

GOOD NEWS ... ONLY?

On the other hand, Jesus cared deeply about relieving both present and eternal suffering.

If Jesus had only cared about the eternal kind, then He would have only preached . . . He wouldn't have healed, raised, fed, listened to, and cared for people. Jesus expected us to also care about both present and eternal suffering (Matthew 25:31-46).

According to Jesus and the apostles, evangelism and social justice are inextricably linked and equally important (Luke 10:25-37; James 1:27-2:26). In other words, they considered this not to be an either/or but rather a both/and issue.

 **PROCESS** – How does the link between the good news and social justice change the way you think about your relationship with others?

SHARING THE GOOD NEWS?

Father John Bettuolucci wrote, "Social action without prayer and conversion to the Lord lacks power and the ability to produce long-lasting change in the socio-economic conditions of the poor. Likewise, prayer and evangelism without social action leads to pietistic withdrawal from the realities of the human condition and an escape from social problems rather than a confrontation and challenge to change."[12]

So, it's important to understand that the structuring of one's character equips an individual to love entirely: God, self, and others. And loving others is not just a message but the care and concern to provide all that is necessary to transform the conditions through relationship.

 **PROCESS** – What opportunities do you have to love others well and in doing so communicate the "good news"?

2.10

MIND
Intellectual

Loving God with your mind means you are learning and growing in knowledge, how to think well about life. This section provides you with knowledge to expand your mind and help you improve your thinking.

EMOTIONAL

HEART – Emotional Processing

Loving God with your heart means you are learning and growing in how to have a healthy emotional life.

RELATIONAL

SOUL – Relational Processing

Loving God with your soul means you are learning and growing in how to have healthy relationships.

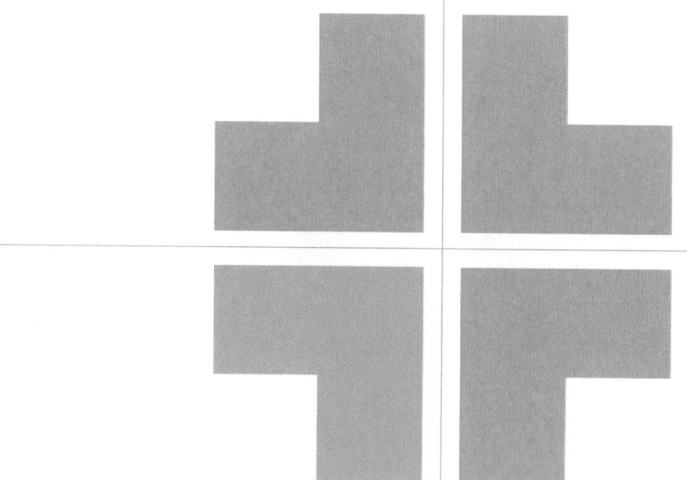

MIND – Intellectual Processing

Loving God with your mind means you are learning and growing in knowledge, how to think well about life.

INTELLECTUAL

STRENGTH – Using Your Influence

Loving God with your strength means you are learning and growing in how to put your unique design into action.

VOCATIONAL

HOW TO THINK ABOUT LIFE

It can be increasingly difficult to think rightly about life in a world that constantly saturates us with information, media, and advertising—literally at the speed of light. So, how do we think about life in such a challenging world?

First, we must have a way of viewing the world. We call this a worldview.

According to James Sire, "A worldview is a commitment, a fundamental orientation of the heart, that can be expressed as a story or in a set of presuppositions which we hold about the basic constitution of reality, and that provides the foundation on which we live and move and have our being."[13]

In short, a worldview is the lens through which we see and interpret the world. What "lens" are you using to see the world?

Everyone has a worldview, whether they're aware of it or not. Worldviews are learned and not inherited, and they develop over time, which makes them very hard to change.

The book *Hidden Worldviews*[14] outlines nine different "lenses," each with a specific focus for living life. As you look at the nine listed below, describe how you see their influence in our world.

1. Individualism - life lived for self

2. Consumerism - life lived for consumption and materialism

3. Nationalism - life lived for country

4. Moral relativism - a life of freedom without authority

5. Scientific naturalism - life explained by science and nature

6. New age - life explained through spiritualism

7. Postmodern tribalism - life with diversity and acceptance

8. Salvation by therapy - life lived to get better

9. Christian theism - life lived in truth and the reality of God's story

 **PROCESS** – Which of the "lenses" above do you most identify with?

DOES THE WAY YOU VIEW THE WORLD WORK?

It's one thing to believe that the way you view the world is correct. It's another thing for that view to actually work.

If you believe that your approach to life works, then wouldn't you naturally be open to having it tested? However, many people do not like to be challenged or tested in what they believe. They become defensive, combative, and sometimes even violent.

As you think through your worldview, keep in mind that for it to be worth embracing it must have evidence (the ability to be tested), be consistent, and make sense.

Take for example moral relativism. If this worldview actually worked, then every person should be able to define for themselves the best way to live. But law stands outside of all of us as an authority. In a morally relative world, we should be able to make our own rules—but we can't. When moral relativism is tested against reality, it does not work.

LIFE

3.1

CHOOSING WISELY

The Scriptures encourage us to "test everything that is said. Hold on to what is good" (1 Thessalonians 5:21).

Testing creates tension and tension is a good thing. When the strings on a guitar are loose, they lack the proper tension to make music. You must be willing to hold the tension of having your worldview tested so you can choose what will last. You must also seek to be wise in what you choose.

It's important to evaluate your own worldview so that you are aware of the way you see the world and how it is different than others' worldviews. You may also be able to spot weaknesses in your worldview and learn to adapt it over time.

3.1

WHAT IS THE BIBLE?

In human history, there is no collection of books that has been scrutinized more than the Bible. It is still the leading bestseller of all time. As literature, it is graphic, poetic, historical, and relevant to societies as well as individuals.

Considered holy by Jews and Christians worldwide, the Bible consists of 66 books originating in three different languages written by 40 contributing authors over a 1,500-year period. The miracle of the Bible is that, regardless of the number of writers involved or the time it took to complete, the message is consistent in revealing God to mankind.

But why should you care?

WHY CAN WE TAKE THE BIBLE SERIOUSLY?

Every day you make moral and ethical decisions. These decisions not only affect you as an individual–they also affect others around you.

How do you evaluate the decisions you have to make? Can you truly make the best decisions possible without outside input?

Taking the Bible seriously begins by understanding that it did not come into being by chance but through a very amazing, intentional process where God interacted with real people and events in human history.

We can trust the Bible as inspired by God, because every book had to meet four important conditions:

1. For the Old Testament, the book needed to be written by a prophet of God. This is important because to be wrong as a prophet would cost you your life. In the New Testament, the book had to be written by someone who actually encountered Jesus Christ, which validates Him as a real historical figure.

2. The book had to be written before 400 BC (Old Testament) or before 100 AD (New Testament).

3. The book had to be in agreement with existing Scripture and teaching.

4. The book had to be recognized and accepted by the early church.*

*Key canons, edicts, and councils include Marcion's Canon (A.D. 140); Muratorian Canon (A.D. 170); Edicts of Diocletian (A.D. 302-305); Council of Hippo (A.D. 393); Council of Carthage (A.D. 397); Council of Trent (A.D. 1546).

The councils referenced above were gatherings where the books and teachings were intensely evaluated, often by hundreds present. Those in attendance tested the authority, history, and manuscripts of each book. Knowing that the Bible experienced such intentional evaluation gives us confidence that what we have and how it came to be was simply miraculous!

 **PROCESS** – Did you know that the Bible had such extensive processes for its formation and testing? How does this change your view of the Bible?

THE BIBLE

3.2

STANDING THE TEST OF TIME

Miraculous events in current history show us the Bible is supernatural and not a religious book of myths. On a regular basis, architectural digs in the Middle East unearth artifacts, locations, and whole cities referenced in the Bible. This affirms that Scripture has physical and historical evidence.

In an article published in *USA Today* on September 6, 2016, experts were excited to find a scroll in En-Gedi (the Dead Sea) dating to the 3rd century and containing the Pentateuch: "To the scholars' astonishment, the newly divulged text is exactly the same, in both letters and format, as text in modern Torah scrolls read by most Jews. 'This is quite amazing for us,' said study co-author Emanuel Tov of the Hebrew University of Jerusalem, 'that in 2,000 years, this text has not changed.'"

Beyond the evidence for the Bible, what is more miraculous is how the teaching continues to change lives worldwide with the message of God's love.

 **PROCESS** – What did you discover about the Bible in this session that you did not know before?

WHY GOD?

The conversation about God today comes with great confusion. We may hear that the concept of God is irrelevant and outdated. But God is the answer without a question in a world where people are looking for answers and starving for meaning. So, why is God an important concept to explore? The simple answer is because God's existence is possible.

There are two kinds of arguments for the existence of God: arguments that do not depend on evidence and arguments that depend on evidence. Sounds pretty logical–right? If God exists, then there should be something we can see that would confirm this is true. But is it necessary to have evidence?

FOR OR AGAINST?

The French philosopher René Descartes believed that the existence of God did not depend on evidence. He concluded that God's existence was necessary because we could conceive the reality of something bigger than ourselves. If God didn't exist, then the thought of Him would never cross your mind. According to Descartes, that is all you need to confirm God's existence.

Others believe that we need evidence to prove God exists. For example, Aristotle and Thomas Aquinas believed there must be a cause for things to exist. For them, that cause is God. The current-day thinker William Lane Craig argues that because there is order and design in the universe, God must exist. German philosopher Immanuel Kant thought God's existence was shown through the presence of moral law in the world. And Soren Kierkegaard suggested that our experience proves God's existence. All of these great minds thought the existence of God was possible but we should have some evidence to prove it.

There are essentially three arguments against the existence of God. Two philosophers who drove the Enlightenment period, John Locke and David Hume, believed that God could not exist because we can't see him. If that is true, then things like atoms, which we could not see before the invention of a microscope, must not have existed before then. Jean-Paul Sartre believed that God did not exist because we do not need him. Epicurus thought that because evil existed in the world, God must not exist.

The importance of understanding the arguments for and against God is simple. When thinking about such a truly important subject as God's existence, it's just responsible to think rightly about it.

 **PROCESS** – How does understanding the arguments for and against God change the way you think about this challenging question?

THE PROBLEM OF EVIL

A poll asked people what one question they would want to ask God if they had the chance, and far and away it was, "Why is there evil and suffering in the world?" The problem of evil is the most common argument used against the existence of God, and rightfully so. Evil is a challenging reality of human existence that is not easy to explain.

The humanist philosopher Paul Draper wrote, "We know that much evil and suffering exists in the world. Christians speak of a personal God who is good, merciful, and all-powerful. This is impossible. God could be good but impotent and thus unable to stop human pain. God could also be sovereign and all-powerful but cruel and unsympathetic to the human condition. God cannot, however, be both good and sovereign. Personally, I don't believe God even exists."

So, is it possible for there to be evil present in the world and for God to exist? When approaching the problem of evil we must consider the following potential views:

"God can do anything He wants."

"We would not know what good is without evil."

"This is the way things are supposed to be."

"All suffering is deserved."

"Evil is useful for producing character."

"Evil is the absence of good."

"Evil is the outcome of man's free choice."

"Evil serves an outcome we cannot see."

 **PROCESS** – How does the detail involved in proving God's existence challenge and encourage you?

WHAT ABOUT THE UNIVERSE?

Why does the universe matter to how we think about life? It's not something we necessarily consider on any given day. Yet our world is inside it and it impacts how we view everything, including our individual lives.

The way you explain the existence of the universe is part of the way you view the world. People attempt to explain the universe in many ways. The Christian view of the world explains it through intelligent design. But another common viewpoint is *naturalism,* which denies a Creator and instead claims that everything evolved through the passing of time and organization of matter. The world and everything in it is nothing but the result of time and chance.

Can life be explained solely by natural processes, or does it require an intelligent designer to explain living systems?

INTELLIGENT DESIGN THEORY

Intelligent design theory (ID) proposes that an intelligent agent acts on nature. The Christian worldview supports intelligent design because we believe that God created the universe.

Intelligent design theory is legitimate because real science is supposed to distinguish between physical and intelligent causes for things. (E.g., forensic science serves to figure out whether something is accidental or purposeful, and archaeology serves to determine if something is naturally formed or intelligently created. The same is true in linguistics, psychology, mathematics, and other studies.)

Intelligent design theory is important because it offers helpful perspectives for thinking about the universe:

1. There is a beginning to space, time, and matter.
2. Certain conditions must exist for life (size of molecules, gravitational fields, distance from sun, etc.).
3. There are groups of parts that will not function without all of their parts (e.g., piano).
4. There are universal moral laws that must originate from somewhere (incest, adultery, violence).
5. Our minds are more than matter.

 **PROCESS** – Which theory do you believe holds greater value in explaining the universe and why—naturalism or intelligent design?

WHY INTELLIGENT DESIGN IS IMPORTANT

If we believe in naturalism, we believe that the world happened at random, and therefore life can have no inherent purpose or meaning and nothing extends beyond the physical world. Without a belief in a Creator and inherent purpose that extends beyond

ourselves, there is very little to drive us or tell us what is right or wrong. The belief in the existence of a Creator gives us reason for morality. It means that we have been created with a purpose in mind and exist as more than just physical beings.

 **PROCESS** – How does the existence of a Creator impact your view of authority and morality? Is this a difficult concept for you to accept?

IS THERE ABSOLUTE TRUTH?

You have heard it said that "You must find your truth," or "Your truth is your truth and my truth is my truth." Some people argue that all religions are really the same. But are they? Are we all scaling the same mountain?

Absolute means perfect and when truth is absolute it is without conflict or flaws. What this also means is that something cannot be absolutely true and not true at the same time. So when it comes to world religions, for them to all be true, they must all teach the same thing—but they don't.

For example, here is what the world religions teach about salvation:

- **Hinduism** claims that salvation is found through a cycle of reincarnations in which one finds the essence of his divine nature. Hinduism teaches that there are some 300,000 gods.

- **Buddhism** asserts that the elimination of "desire" leads to peace of mind and ultimate salvation. Buddhism teaches that there is no god.

- **Islam** teaches that one must obey God's laws in hope that the good deeds will outweigh the bad. Islam teaches that there is one god, Allah.

- **Christianity** teaches that salvation comes by faith in the sacrifice of Jesus on the cross for our sins, providing God's unmerited grace. Christianity teaches that there is one triune God.

 **PROCESS** – Does the description of absolute truth above resonate with what you already believe or does it create tension for you?

WHO IS RIGHT?

Discovering where the truth is found can be a very challenging but important endeavor. Finding the truth is easiest by learning how to think about it. Logic can help us tremendously.

There are three basic laws of logic:

1. The law of identity (something is itself and not something else)

2. The law of the excluded middle (something cannot partially exist)

3. The law of non-contradiction (something cannot exist *and* not exist at the same time)

Apply these laws to the claims of the major world religions, and it is logically impossible for all religions to be right since they make incompatible claims:

- **Hindu Vedas:** *"Truth* is one, but the sages speak of it in many different ways."

- **Buddha:** "My teaching points the way to the attainment of *truth."*

- **Muhammad:** "The *truth* has been revealed to me."

- **Jesus:** "I am the truth" (John 14:6).

Not all of these statements can be right because they contradict each other. There cannot be only one truth and many truths at the same time.

JESUS

Jesus distinguishes himself from other religious leaders by claiming not just to know the truth or point the way toward truth but to actually personify the truth. He goes on to explicitly say that no one can come to God except through Him. So, the center of the Christian faith is Jesus . . . If we remove Jesus, there is no Christianity. If we trust the Bible, Jesus is the truth, so no other religion can logically be true.

"I am the way, the truth, and the life. No one can come to the Father except through me" (John 14:6).

"There is salvation in no one else! God has given no other name under heaven by which we must be saved" (Acts 4:12).

 **PROCESS** – How do the laws of logic help you to think about the truth claims of Jesus and the reality of the Christian faith?

WHY ARE HUMANS VALUABLE?

As humans, we are either an accident or created with a purpose. There is no in between. It is impossible to argue that human beings are accidental and still possesses a purpose without undermining value. Take for instance a dollar bill. The reason it is called a dollar is because it possesses a specific value that performs a function directly tied to its value.

As human beings, where do we derive our value?

"Then God said, 'Let us make human beings in our image, to be like us. They will reign over the fish in the sea, the birds in the sky, the livestock, all the wild animals on the earth, and the small animals that scurry along the ground.' So God created human beings in his own image. In the image of God he created them; male and female he created them."

–Genesis 1:26-27

Did you know you were made in the image of God? Made to reflect every aspect of the rich relationship the Father, Son, and Holy Spirit share? Being made in the image of God is not only something to be cherished, it also comes with responsibility.

Unfortunately, the fall of man (Genesis 3) corrupted the reflection of God in us. Though the image of God was tarnished by the fall, it was not lost.

LIVING A VALUABLE LIFE

When you understand the value of being made in the image of God, life takes on new meaning. Life is no longer an accident that you're trying to make sense of. Instead, it becomes a journey rich with meaning and fulfillment as you live out of the purpose God has designed for you.

Living out the image of God provides us first with great responsibility (Genesis 2:15) as those who care for His creation. It also means that we are not alone. Relationships are one of the primary ways we experience Him as we connect to one another through His image in us (Genesis 2:18). In relationship is where we see the qualities of God revealed (Genesis 1:26) and this is a tremendous encouragement to our lives. (Genesis 1:28)

 **PROCESS** – As you consider the description of living life bearing God's image, write about how this can impact your life.

BEARING THE IMAGE OF GOD AS A COMMUNITY

Though the image of God in us was corrupted, it is being restored daily until we are fully conformed into the image of Christ in glory (Colossians 3:9-10; Romans 12:2). This brings us hope and encourages us in our daily living as we work toward becoming closer to the image of Christ. As a result, we can now live together in a community where God's image is fully realized (Genesis 1:26-27).

God made us in His image to set us apart from all other creatures so we could have relationship with Him and each other (Genesis 1:28) and this is what allows us to have a healthy self-image (Genesis 1:31; 1 Corinthians 11:7).

HUMANITY

3.6

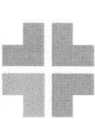

It gives us a deep sense of meaning to live out of God's image the way we were designed (Genesis 2:15) as men and women play the roles God created for them (Genesis 5:1-2). Living in God's image gives all of human life dignity (Genesis 9:6; James 3:9).

 **PROCESS** – From your perspective, how can the description above of community reflecting God's image make our world a better place?

ARE YOU A GOOD PERSON?

When we talk about ethics, we are speaking about moral actions. Interpreting the ethics of a moral action involves examining the intent, motive, and means of whoever is performing the action.

So how do we know if something is right or wrong?

There are three primary views about moral actions. First, there is the belief that some things are true whether or not anyone believes they are and these truths can be applied to all people and circumstances. Next is the belief that every individual ought to act in accordance with their society's moral code. Some people call this a social contract or a socially agreed-upon standard. Last is the belief that moral truth does not exist.

Morality is important because it affects the way we see other people and how we live among each other. If there is no defined right or wrong, how can we know what is actually good?

THE PROBLEMS WITH MORAL RELATIVISM

Moral relativism is simply the belief that each person can determine on their own what is right and wrong.

The strongest argument against moral relativism is if the social moral code is always right, then there is never justification for moral reform. You can imagine how this can be a problem since there are cultures where slavery is acceptable. How would everyone come against slavery if the code is always viewed as right? Similarly, if individual relativism is true, then no one can grow morally or improve their moral behavior or beliefs.

 **PROCESS** – Describe how you have seen moral relativism encouraged by our society. What problems has this caused from your perspective?

WHEN SOCIETY DESTROYS ITSELF

Moral truth and moral law exist because they come from God. This gives us a higher power to which we are accountable. Without it, there would be no objective truth. Today, there is an intellectual movement called deconstructionism that seeks to undermine this important concept.

Jacques Derrida, the French intellectual, is known as the "Father of Deconstructionism." Deconstructionism is the view that the meanings of words are completely arbitrary and reality is essentially unknowable, so nothing can actually be true.

Roger Kimball wrote, "Deconstruction promises its adherents not only emancipation from the responsibilities of truth but also the prospect of engaging in a species of radical activism. A blow against the legitimacy of language is at the same time a blow against the legitimacy of the tradition in which language lives and has meaning. By undercutting the idea of truth, the deconstructionist also undercuts the idea of value, including established social and moral values."[15] His point is Derrida's deconstructionism fundamentally undermines any claims to absolute truth.

According to Scripture, moral truth matters and there are things we *must* believe and do.

"For God is Spirit, so those who worship him *must* worship in spirit and in truth" (John 4:24).

PROCESS – List some of the risks you find with believing that words can be changed to mean whatever a person decides they should mean.

WHAT IS KNOWLEDGE?

Knowledge is defined as "an acquaintance with facts, truths, or principles, as from study or investigation." It's important to understand that knowledge is not the same as information. Knowledge is acquired by spending time with information and getting to know how parts tie together in a meaningful way.

Knowledge is important because it helps us interpret the world. Without knowledge we would not be able to identify whether something is true.

How do we know what we know? The study of how things can be known is called epistemology, which is a branch of philosophy that studies the nature of knowledge.

Following is the history of epistemology that shows some important changes over time:

1. Premodern era (<1650): "There is divine truth and we can know it."
2. Modern era (1650-1950): "There is no divine truth and we can know it."
3. Postmodern era (>1950): "There is no divine truth and we cannot know it."

Our culture is influenced by postmodern thought. The postmodern era has sought to eliminate the ability for divine or supernatural knowledge to exist. It's important to understand how postmodernism influences contemporary thought so you can identify issues in our culture that stem from this philosophy.

THE DANGERS OF POSTMODERNISM

Postmodernism is a philosophical movement away from the belief in truth and existence of God. Postmodernists believe we cannot know things as they really are but only as they appear to us. Practically, this leads to a belief that religion or theology is completely a "social construction."

Postmodernism seeks to remove meaning from words and language so that nothing can be consistently defined. If we cannot be sure of what words mean, then how can we truly know anything? This is the single goal of postmodernism. This can lead to other problems because, without objective truth, there is no moral truth. If there is no inherent meaning, people lack purpose.

 **PROCESS** – How have you seen the effects of postmodernism in our culture? What future problems do you think can develop because of this philosophy?

A CHRISTIAN RESPONSE TO POSTMODERNISM

Is it possible to be confident about something without being certain? For example, are you confident that you will wake up tomorrow morning? Most likely this is going to happen, but can you be 100 percent certain about it? No. But you don't have to be certain that it will occur to be confident that it will.

Christianity's response to postmodernism is to promote this kind of perspective. We can stand on the foundation of what has been true in the past and what works even though there cannot be utter certainty. In other words, we don't have to be certain about something in order to believe it (Hebrews 11:1,6). The great Christian thinker Martin Luther said, "Faith is a living and unshakable confidence, a belief in the grace of God so assured that a man would die a thousand deaths for its sake!"[16]

PROCESS – How confident are you in the existence of God without being certain? Is this a challenging or easy concept for you to accept?

CULTURE AND PURPOSE

Finding a deeper sense of meaning is a central focus today for many people. But how we find a greater depth of meaning in life is directly related to how we interact with culture.

Culture is all around us. However, sometimes it can be difficult to understand the effects of culture as it grows and changes. A simple definition for culture is the quality in a person or society that arises from a concern for what is excellent in arts, letters, manners, scholarly pursuits, and values.

There are two ways of interacting with culture: either through our senses or with ideas.

Those who believe one can only interact with culture through senses believe their own experiences and observations are the only things that are valuable. These kinds of cultures do not last because they are not able to answer life's most fundamental questions: Is there a God? Is there life after death? Is there a purpose in life? Such cultures only accept what is visible and scientific. As a result, anything unseen holds no value.

Around 1930, American culture split apart faith and reason to become a culture driven by senses, and the consequence of living in this kind of culture is that life is meaningless and futile. In other words, there is no meaning or purpose.

Interacting with culture through ideas presents a whole different point of view. This kind of culture finds value in all things not just because they can be observed or used. There is right and wrong, not just good and bad, and this results in depth of purpose and meaning.

HOW PURPOSE FUNCTIONS

When we talk about purpose, we are speaking about where our actions are going and why. We must consider the direction our actions are taking us and how or why we view things the way we do. In cultures based on senses, there is *no* direction, so there is *no* purpose in anything! Sense-based cultures value only things that serve some kind of end. Things are not valuable simply because they exist.

In cultures driven by ideas, everything has a purpose and value and thus requires us to think about how we interact with all things in our surroundings. Ultimately, purpose is tied to what is good.

Today there are three common misconceptions for determining if something is good. First is hedonism, the idea that if it provides pleasure it must be good. Next is pluralism, which claims there are many ways of understanding what is good. Last is rationalism, the belief that only reason can tell us what is good.

 **PROCESS** – Which of the three misconceptions do you see most at work in our culture today?

CULTURE WITH PURPOSE PROVIDES MEANING

When we interact with culture through ideas, we become open to finding meaning rather than just using things around us for our own pleasure. Life becomes about what is right. In other words, something can be done for a purpose bigger than serving ourselves.

MEANING

3.9

Christians, therefore, believe that the ends do ***not*** justify the means because people, actions, and causes have intrinsic value. There is purpose and meaning to everything.

PROCESS – How do you need to change the way you interact with culture to find a deeper sense of meaning?

3.9

WHAT IS SEXUALITY?

Sexuality is much more than sex—it refers to our entire identity as human beings.

In a treatise on sexuality, the American Lutheran Church stated, "Human sexuality includes all we are as human beings. Sexuality, at the very least, is biological, psychological, cultural, social, and spiritual. To be a person is to be a sexual being."[17]

The late theologian Stanley Grenz wrote, "Sexuality refers to our fundamental existence as males or females."[18]

The Bible summarizes creation by telling us that God made humans male and female. Scripture also implies that the two sexes are distinctly different so they complement each other. Therefore, our sexuality affects virtually all of our social interactions and relationships.

THE FOUNDATION OF OUR SEXUALITY

Our sexuality as humans is based upon the example of the Triune God. The three members of the Trinity exist in harmony and communion with one another. Therefore, we are reflecting God's image when we are in relationship with others. Because of this connection, human sexuality is for the purpose of creating intimacy. Separating sexuality from true intimacy is a distortion of God's design.

Because sex is such a powerful expression of our sexuality, Scripture places a high value and significance upon sexual faithfulness. At the same time, Scripture strongly condemns all forms of sexual unfaithfulness. The Bible clearly states that sexual sin is unlike any other physical act because it alone creates a mystical and permanent union between two people.

 **PROCESS** – In your own words, write about why you believe sexual faithfulness is important in a relationship.

SEXUALITY, MARRIAGE, AND SINGLENESS

C.S Lewis said, "The truth is that whenever a man lies with a woman, there, whether they like it or not, a transcendental relation is set up between them which must be eternally enjoyed or eternally endured." For this reason, Scripture restricts sexual intimacy to lifetime marriage between one man and one woman.

In Genesis, God created two sexually distinct human beings, intended to procreate and designed to literally fit together and become one. God intends that union to be a permanent relationship (Matthew 19:4-6) and to be exclusive and monogamous (Hebrews 13:4). That means all sexual activity outside of the marital union is immoral in God's eyes (1 Corinthians 6:16-18).

The other biblical model of sexuality is singleness (1 Corinthians 7:32-35). Jesus, Paul, and many others in Scripture conducted lives dedicated to God and remained single. It is important to know that marriage is not the only way to honor God with our sexuality.

SEXUALITY

3.10

 **PROCESS** – Interact below with your own views on sexuality and what has been refer-
enced above. Why do you believe it is important for God's design to be
shown through our sexuality?

STRENGTH
Vocational

Loving God with your strength means you are learning and growing in how to put your unique design into action. This section will help you understand your own strengths and find ways to improve them.

EMOTIONAL

HEART – Emotional Processing

Loving God with your heart means you are learning and growing in how to have a healthy emotional life.

RELATIONAL

SOUL – Relational Processing

Loving God with your soul means you are learning and growing in how to have healthy relationships.

MIND – Intellectual Processing

Loving God with your mind means you are learning and growing in knowledge, how to think well about life.

INTELLECTUAL

STRENGTH – Using Your Influence

Loving God with your strength means you are learning and growing in how to put your unique design into action.

VOCATIONAL

WHAT IS SELF-IMAGE?

Your self-image is the view or value you have for yourself.

The reason having a healthy self-image is so important is because it's an expression of how we understand who we are and what we've been made to do. But today there is so much confusion in the world around us that it can be difficult to know what to believe about ourselves.

The Boston College Christian professor and philosopher Peter Kreeft wrote, "There is a deep spiritual sorrow at the heart of modern civilization because it is the first civilization in all of history that does not know who it is or why it is, that cannot answer the three great questions: Where did I come from? Why am I here? And, where am I going? This is the most terrifying thing of all to us because our primary need is denied, our need for meaning."[19]

This is a very important perspective—our need to see ourselves as valuable and our need to recognize our ability to contribute something meaningful to this life. But to have a healthy and strong self-image we must understand how it is directly connected to our identity and purpose.

IDENTITY, PURPOSE, AND SELF-IMAGE

Identity can be summarized as the character or qualities that make someone or something what it is.

We should take the concept of identity seriously because if something cannot be identified, it loses its value all together. This is why it is critical for us to have a clear sense of identity, because what makes up our identity directly contributes to our sense of worth.

In a sense, your identity is a story. It combines where you came from with what you're good at and what or who has influenced you. Understanding this about identity provides us clues to where we can find a deep sense of meaning and purpose.

The search for meaning is a primary issue in our world today. So, where do we go to find it? Disney? Money? Success? Fame? Many have tried these and more in an effort to find their place in the world, but there is only one solution—God.

Simply being made in God's image gives us all great purpose.

 **PROCESS** – Where have you tried to find meaning and purpose in life aside from God?

DIGNITY AND EQUALITY

We have value and worth because we are made in the Image of God (Genesis 1:26-27). The ancient language of Hebrew lets us know that being made in God's image means we are a direct representation of the nature the Father, Son, and Holy Spirit share. We cannot find a deeper sense of meaning than *that*.

C.S. Lewis said, "There are no ordinary people. You have never talked to a mere mortal."[20]

John Jefferson Davis wrote, "God's creation is immense but man, as the crown of creation, has a dignity and grandeur that surpasses that of the cosmos."[21]

Lewis and Davis help us see that every human has value because the image of God in every person gives them worth. As a result, we must realize that treating ourselves and others with dignity is incredibly important. It also helps us see that equality is directly related to dignity as well.

If we do not have a clear sense of how valuable we really are, it is difficult to see that same value in others. Having a strong self-image derived from a God-given identity and purpose ultimately influences how we see others and the rest of the world.

 **PROCESS** – How do the perspectives from Lewis and Davis influence your view on dignity and equality?

HOW WE THINK MATTERS

God gives each of us strengths and weaknesses. How you think about your strengths and weaknesses makes a huge difference. It can be easy to fixate on how others are better than you in one area or another, or to focus on things that you do poorly. But this kind of thinking isn't productive and can harm you in the long run.

According to Christian neuro-psychologist Dr. Caroline Leaf, research overwhelmingly shows that we can change the shape of our DNA with our thoughts. Scientific research reveals that 87-98 percent of all mental and physical illness is linked to thought life.

What this tells us is how we think matters, and what we think about matters too. Ralph Waldo Emerson said, "Life consists of what a man is thinking about all day."

Author James Allen put it this way: "You are today where your thoughts have brought you. You will be tomorrow where your thoughts take you."

"And now, dear brothers and sisters, one final thing. Fix your thoughts on what is true, and honorable, and right, and pure, and lovely, and admirable. Think about things that are excellent and worthy of praise" (Philippians 4:8).

How we think about life matters, and yet we often focus and fixate on the *wrong things.* Instead, focus on your strengths. For the Scriptures tell us, "As a man thinks in his heart, so is he" (Proverbs 23:7, NKJV).

 **PROCESS** – List one thought in your life you would like to stop fixating on. What would be the benefits?

FOCUS ON YOUR STRENGTHS

When we focus on our weaknesses, we spend time, energy, and resources on shoring up qualities that will never be strengths–when we could instead invest in and maximize what we do well.

Leaders are always pushing to grow, develop, and optimize their abilities. Isaiah 54:2 (ESV) encourages this mindset when it says, "Enlarge the place of your tent, and let the curtains of your habitations be stretched out; do not hold back; lengthen your cords and strengthen your stakes."

Dr. John Townsend recommends using an "open stance system" by always being open to learning, forging new and deeper relationships, and seeking out new opportunities for growth.

 **PROCESS** – What are your strengths? How can you leverage them?

DISCOVERING YOUR STRENGTHS

If you have a difficult time identifying your strengths, there are a number of steps that can help. Try taking a strengths assessment or inventory, such as StrengthsFinder. If you want personalized guidance, find a coach who can help you create a plan. Look for ways to leverage your strengths and set goals that will stretch your capacity.

 **PROCESS** – Which of the above recommendations would help you the most in leveraging your strengths? When will you set out to do it?

4.2

WHY SET GOALS?

"By reaching for what appears to be the impossible, we often actually do the impossible. And even when we do not quite make it, we inevitably wind up doing much better than we would have done."

–Jack Welch

For years, Dupont had a goal of "zero accidents," and though they never reached that goal, their accident rate decreased and was significantly lower than other companies. When President Kennedy set a goal in the 1960s to reach the moon, the technology did not exist to do it. Without goals, especially ones that stretch us, we will never reach our capacity or be our best.

Zig Ziglar famously said, "If you aim at nothing, you will hit it every time."

Goal setting is about aiming . . . aiming at a target that is far away and seemingly out of reach.

Through the process of reaching your goals, you'll learn things about yourself and begin to understand yourself at deeper levels. You will refine and expand your priorities by discovering what is most important to you. You will identify your preferred future, and when you learn to set and achieve your goals, you'll be able to align the trajectory of your life to achieve the future you want.

 **PROCESS** – Are you a goal setter? Why or why not?

HOW TO SET A GOAL

Everyone interacts with goals differently and there is not a "one size fits all" approach. So you must spend time exploring different ways to set goals to find what works best for you. A place to start is to consider setting SMART goals:

Specific–What precisely are you hoping to achieve?

Measurable–How do you know when you will have achieved it?

Attainable–Are you realistically capable of achieving this goal?

Relevant–How does this goal help you achieve what you want?

Timely–Is there an expiration date for what you want to achieve?

 **PROCESS** – Think about something you would like to achieve in the near future and practice writing a SMART goal.

SETTING STRETCH GOALS

A stretch goal is bigger than the average goal. It is not achievable easily or quickly, and it often requires diligent planning and dedication. It is meant to stretch you further than you can currently go, and you often cannot get there on your own.

GOALS

4.3

However, when you accomplish a stretch goal, growth occurs and your capacity is deepened! There is real and lasting satisfaction in setting and achieving stretch goals.

So, how do you do it?

1. Think about something you desire and hope to achieve, personally or professionally, within the next year (limit yourself to three stretch goals).

2. Write it down in a single sentence.

3. On a scale of 1 to 10, assign a number to where you are now toward achieving this goal.

4. Create a plan for achieving the goal(s) with action steps.

5. Track your progress on a weekly or monthly basis.

 **PROCESS** – Who are two people in your life you think would help encourage you to reach your goals?

THE IMPORTANCE OF NEEDS

There are different kinds of human needs.

For example, every person needs food, water, and oxygen to survive—these are called physical needs. But we also have needs that can only be met by being in relationship with others. Relational needs help us feel safe and cared for by others, but we often don't admit to having them.

Why is it so hard to think about our own needs? And why is it even harder to ask for them?

Some think that asking for what we need relationally is somehow weak. But asking for what we need from others is healthy and necessary.

We are responsible for meeting our own needs. Although we would love for others to know what we need and provide it for us, it is unrealistic to expect that to happen.

MEETING YOUR NEEDS

Because others are not responsible for your needs, you must take responsibility for yourself.

That being the case, there are two steps to getting your needs met:

Identifying the Need ("I Need . . . ")

Identifying what you need can be challenging simply because we often don't know how to communicate our needs. So having the language for our needs is incredibly helpful.

A way to begin bringing language to what you need is by answering the "I need . . ." question. Here are some examples:

- "I need to be heard."
- "I need to be encouraged."
- "I need feedback."
- "I need perspective."

Once you have learned how to describe what you need, it becomes much easier to ask someone to provide it for you.

PROCESS – What needs do you have that you can identify? Identify two or three right now:

1. _____ 2. _____ 3. _____

Asking for the Need ("I need you to . . . ")

Identifying our needs is only half of the challenge. Mustering the courage to ask others to help is the other half. Our needs will never be met if we don't ask.

HOW DO YOU ASK?

- Identify your need.
- Ask for what you need.
- Accept the help.
- Process the good.

We should not hesitate to ask others to help us because we are designed and intended by God to meet one another's needs.

In the New Testament, there are 59 "one another" statements, so this suggests that meeting one another's needs is **the** primary activity of the church.

 **PROCESS** – Who is someone you trust who can help you with one of the needs you listed above?

THE IMPORTANCE OF VALUES

What are your values? What are your guiding principles or core convictions in life?

Everyone has a set of core values, whether they can articulate them or not. What makes certain values "core" values is how important and central they are to you. The dictionary defines core values as "the fundamental beliefs of a person or an organization."

Core values are vital because they support your vision, shape your identity, and help you sustain momentum.

HOW TO CREATE YOUR CORE VALUES

This exercise will help you create a list of core values for yourself or for a team.

1. Brainstorm by asking yourself probing questions:

    A. What am I best at?

    B. What do I care most about?

    C. What impact do I want to have?

    D. What things will I not compromise?

    E. What do I want to be known for?

2. Write down what comes to mind in single words or short phrases.

3. Organize, prioritize, and narrow your list to the top five.

4. Check your list with trusted advisors for feedback. If you're creating core values for a team, consult with team members.

 **PROCESS** – Why do you think having clear core values is important for individuals and teams?

SHAPING HEALTHY CULTURE

Peter Drucker famously declared, "Culture eats strategy for breakfast."

The reason core values are so important is they shape *culture.*

We cannot overstate the importance of building healthy culture in all dimensions of life. The character structuring process you have been learning in the *Four Dimensions of Human Health* has been developed for that sole purpose.

According to Dr. John Townsend, core values are the "gut" of every person and organization, and they are the driver for everything we do.[22]

In order to create and sustain desirable culture, we must integrate our core values into life. The more we see and think about them, the quicker they begin to influence our life in all dimensions. Our recommendation is to write out your core values, *rehearse them on a regular basis*, and *display them* in a place where they visually capture your attention.

Be creative!

PROCESS – Brainstorm a way you can display your core values so that you see them often.

4.5

WHAT IS RESPONSIBILITY?

"Maturity doesn't come with age; it comes with acceptance of responsibility."

—Ed Cole

What is responsibility? And how does one get it?

The word responsibility comes from the Latin root **responsus,** which means to respond. So to be responsible is about responding or being responsive . . . but to what?

Responsibility is directly related to how we manage the demands that are placed on our lives. We are responsive to the demands of life when we live up to them and are able to meet them. If we find that we are not able to meet them, responsibility then becomes an opportunity for growth.

Responsibility is earned, not deserved. In other words, we are not given responsibility without first doing something to prove ourselves!

The reality of life is that you are responsible for many things. The question is whether or not you care.

 **PROCESS** – How have you learned responsibility up to this point in your life? Are there any areas where you feel like to need to take more responsibility?

ACCEPTING AND TAKING RESPONSIBILITY

"Accepting" responsibility and "taking" responsibility are two different things.

Accepting responsibility is passive, while taking is proactive, which means not waiting for responsibility to come to you but rather going to get it.

Responsibility is about three things:

1. Ownership – the capacity to act independently and make decisions
2. Accountability – the capacity to receive evaluation and accept blame
3. Authority – the capacity to meet obligations and fulfill duties

 **PROCESS** – What do the following passages teach us about responsibility? Genesis 3:8-13; Acts 8:32-33; James 1:12-15.

SECOND-LEVEL RESPONSIBILITY

"Second-level responsibility" is about taking on *more* responsibility, not just for yourself but also for others (e.g., coaches, generals, pastors, bosses, teachers, parents, and other leadership roles). It shows we have the ability to carry the weight of what is being asked of us. Augustine said, "God provides the wind, but man must raise the sails."

In order to move from level one to level two, you can become more responsible by taking more initiative, becoming more decisive, asking for more responsibility, taking more risks, and accepting more challenges.

Being able to take on more responsibility is a tremendous asset, but it can also be a drawback. We must evaluate our capacity so that the responsibility we take on doesn't cause us to compromise other dimensions of our lives (e.g., relationships).

Responsibility is an opportunity that allows us to reflect God's glory through leading on behalf of others, but we must do it with wisdom and humility.

WHAT IS RESILIENCE?

"Humankind cannot stand very much reality."

–T.S. Eliot

There are two kinds of reality: positive (prosperity) and negative (adversity). We need to understand these truths about adversity:

- Adversity is real.
- Adversity is common.
- Adversity isn't always bad.
- Adversity can be overcome.

The Bible says adversity is meant to "test" us (James 1:3; 1 Peter 4:12). And in ancient Greek, the word for "test" refers to trying something in order to prove its resilience. It means to pound, prod, push, and pull something beyond its limits to see if it bounces back.

The Oxford Dictionary defines resilience as "the capacity to recover quickly from difficulties and the ability of a substance or object to regain its shape."

HOW TO DEVELOP RESILIENCE

Resilience is an ability or capacity, which suggests that it can be developed and deepened. Helen Keller said, "Although the world is full of suffering, it is also full of the overcoming of it."

Someone once asked C.S. Lewis, "Why do the righteous suffer?" "Why not?" he replied. "They're the only ones who can take it."

If you would like to become more resilient, consider how the following perspectives can assist in that process:

- Accept that adversity will happen in your life.
- Avoid harsh treatment of yourself (especially during trials).
- Remember what is true, good, and beautiful.
- Choose to forgive.
- Stay in connected relationships.

 **PROCESS** – Which of these five actions can help you most to become more resilient?

GOODNESS IN ADVERSITY

Adversity *can* actually be good, and the Scriptures have much to say about this topic. In fact, it is possible to be happy in adversity!

"God blesses you when people mock you and persecute you and lie about you and say all sorts of evil things against you because you are my followers. Be happy about it! Be very glad! For a great reward awaits you in heaven. And remember, the ancient prophets were persecuted in the same way" (Matthew 5:11-12).

RESILIENCE

4.7

"God blesses those who patiently endure testing and temptation . . ." (James 1:12).

"But even if you suffer for doing what is right, God will reward you for it . . . If you are insulted because you bear the name of Christ, you will be blessed, for the glorious Spirit of God[a] rests upon you" (1 Peter 3:14; 4:14).

This does not mean a person should always be happy in adversity. But adversity often has good implications for our lives and it will contribute to our overall sense of well-being when it is allowed to do its work.

 **PROCESS** – Why do you think adversity can be good? What value is there in adversity for us?

WHAT IS RHYTHM?

"Every now and then go away, have a little relaxation, for when you come back to your work your judgment will be surer. Go some distance away because then the work appears smaller and more of it can be taken in at a glance and a lack of harmony and proportion is more readily seen."

–Leonardo da Vinci

Everyone needs to step back, relax, and restore. We need weekends and vacations. We were not designed to go without breaks, and without them we will wear down, become exhausted, get sick, and eventually die.

God had specific intentions for human beings when He made us, and we need to pay attention to the significance of that reality. He meant for us to have a rhythm in our lives, to hold to a regular, repeated cycle of activity and relaxation–and doing so comes with great benefit. We must create space in our lives in order to accommodate the unexpected, maintain a healthy tension between work and life, and carve out time for regular breaks from labor.

A MODEL FOR RHYTHM

God modeled for us the rhythm of life He wants us to follow, in which we work for six days and rest on the seventh.

Genesis 2:1-3: "On the seventh day God had finished his work of creation, so he rested from all his work. And God blessed the seventh day and declared it holy, because it was the day when he rested from all his work of creation."

In Hebrew, "rest" means to cease or desist from one's regular duty or activity. So, resting means to step away from whatever we do at least one day each week.

The Hebrew word for "blessed" means to sanctify something or make it holy. Therefore, taking time to rest is not an optional thing for us. It is an ordained command designed for our goodness and well-being.

 **PROCESS** – Why do you think God ***commands*** us to rest?

DEVELOPING A RHYTHM

Gordon MacDonald wrote, "Does God indeed need to rest? Of course not! But did God choose to rest? Yes. Why? Because God subjected creation to a rhythm of rest and work that He revealed by observing the rhythm Himself, as a precedent for everyone else. In this way, He showed us a key to order in our private worlds."[23]

Developing a rhythm takes experimentation. You must discover the places, activities, and periods of time that provide rest for you.

One key element that's often overlooked is simply getting the right amount of sleep. God has designed the body to repair and recharge itself, but it cannot perform this function if we do not provide it enough time. While work is good and honoring to God, it can cause us great grief if we do not find a rhythm that includes rest.

 **PROCESS** – What can we learn about the rhythm of life from the following passages? Mark 1:35; Mark 2:27; Mark 6:30-31; Matthew 11:28-29.

WHAT IS AWARENESS?

David Foster Wallace, in his famous commencement speech at Kenyon College in 2005, said, "The real value of a real education has almost nothing to do with knowledge and everything to do with simple awareness; awareness of what is so real and essential, so hidden in plain sight all around us, all the time, that we have to keep reminding ourselves over and over."

What is awareness? Awareness is the skill to read and address a situation. For example, you become aware that your friend is struggling with anxiety. Now you have knowledge you didn't have before. But what will you do with that knowledge? Awareness applies knowledge and seeks ways to help.

However, being aware of what is going on around you is not the only kind of awareness. You must also be aware of what is going on within yourself.

Awareness is an emotional skill that benefits all of the environments we influence. Awareness is related to emotional intelligence (EI or EQ) and designed to benefit our ability to be in tune with life, ourselves, and others.

 **PROCESS** – When was a time in the past when you became aware of something with a friend or yourself and addressed the situation in a helpful way?

EMOTIONAL INTELLIGENCE (EQ)

Emotional intelligence is "the capacity to be aware of, control, and express one's emotions, and to handle interpersonal relationships judiciously and empathetically."

In practical terms, emotional intelligence is about being aware of how emotions drive our behavior and impact others positively or negatively, and learning how to manage those emotions–both our own and others'–especially when we are under pressure.

- Self-awareness is *understanding* and *regulating* one's own emotions.
- Social awareness is *reading* and *responding* to other people's emotions.

Taken together, awareness is about how we experience others and how others experience us. It is about zeroing in on the tiny nuances of conversation, tone, posture, body language, and energy in a room.

GROWING YOUR AWARENESS

People with great awareness can pick up on the slightest disturbance in a room with intuitive perception. It's a natural gift for some, but for most, it is a skill that must be developed.

So, how can you grow in your awareness?

Attune to what is happening around you and pay attention to others to sense what they are feeling. It may not always be easy to pick up on emotions around you or to understand your own emotions. You can use assessment tools to identify gaps in your emotional intelligence.

As you make progress, ask friends and family for honest feedback and adjust accordingly. Work on developing your skills like focused listening and empathy (feeling *with*).

AWARENESS

4.9

You can enlist the services of a coach to give you personalized feedback and advice, or you can attend leadership training and read relevant books and research.

In the public and the professional arena, emotional intelligence (EQ) is now considered more important, more desirable, and more valuable than cognitive intelligence (IQ)!

 **PROCESS** – What immediate benefit do you think you would experience by growing your level of awareness?

UNDERSTANDING VOCATION

The English word "vocation" comes from the Latin word *vocare*, which means "to call or summon," and refers to the work a person is called to by God.

We sometimes refer to our work as a "calling" because God has called us to do it. In other words, our work is not just a job. It is a profession with a purpose. What makes a profession a "vocation" is a sense of divine assignment to what we do.

It involves hearing the voice of God about what He is calling us to do. Hearing His call can be difficult because God's voice is not the only one calling to us. His voice often gets drowned out by the other voices around us.

As Frederick Buechner wrote, "There are all different kinds of voices calling you to all different kinds of work, and the problem is to find out which is the voice of God rather than of Society, say, or the Superego, or Self-Interest."[24]

The question is whether we are hearing God, ourselves, or somebody else when it comes to our chosen profession. God has plans for us, but so do we, and so do others.

FINDING YOUR VOCATION

So, how can you tune into the voice of God to know his plan for you?

Buechner explained how to hear God: "By and large a good rule for finding out is this: the kind of work God usually calls you to is the kind of work (a) that you need most to do and (b) that the world most needs to have done. 'The place God calls you to is the place where your deep gladness and the world's deep hunger meet.'"[25]

According to Buechner, a good way to think about your calling is looking for the intersection between your passion and the world's need. In other words, you must look inward *and* outward.

Finding your vocation involves looking for and following the road signs:

1. Bible
2. Inner witness
3. Personal desires
4. Circumstance
5. Mature counsel
6. Common sense
7. Special guidance

 **PROCESS** – Do the road signs agree? Are doors opening? Do others confirm? Do you feel peace? (Scriptures: Psalm 32:8; Proverbs 3:5-6; P roverbs 16:9; Romans 12:2; Ephesians 5:17; 6:6; Colossians 1:9; 4:12.)

CONCLUSION

Now that you have experienced how the *Four Dimensions of Human Health* create a structure for integrating love into your life, the challenge is to continue. We hope the sessions contained within this guide helped you see a way of approaching life that brings color and context to your thoughts, feelings, and actions. As we said at the beginning, love is not just an emotion. It is foundational and structural in providing architecture for all of life.

A life oriented by love is a moment-by-moment decision lived out daily. And you must understand that learning to love well, as the person God designed you to be, will take time and effort. Just like you have already invested in the *Four Dimensions of Human Health* experience, you will need to continue that same approach going forward. We encourage you to revisit this guide often as it is not designed as a one-time learning opportunity. Instead, it's a tool that you will source to maintain a balanced life.

The road ahead will be challenging. You may experience great struggle and even suffering as you seek to live a life where love is fully integrated. When those times occur, we hope you will draw courage and comfort, as we do, from Romans 5:3-5:

"We can rejoice, too, when we run into problems and trials, for we know that they help us develop endurance. And endurance develops strength of character, and character strengthens our confident hope of salvation. And this hope will not lead to disappointment. For we know how dearly God loves us, because he has given us the Holy Spirit to fill our hearts with his love."

If there is any way we can help you along your journey do not hesitate to reach out to us at the Love and Transformation Institute through email (Info@LoveandTransformation.org) or our website (LoveandTransformation.org). We would love to hear from you!

Love well!
Ben Bost and Kent DelHousaye

END NOTES AND REFERENCES

1. Alister McGrath, *Christian Theology: An Introduction,* 3rd ed. (London: Blackwell, 2001), 325.

2. Tim Keller, *The Reason for God: Belief in an age of Skepticism* (New York: Penguin Books, 2008), 215.

3. David Brooks, *The Road to Character* (New York: Random House, 2015), 257.

4. Henry Cloud and John Townsend, *Boundaries* (Grand Rapids: Zondervan, 1992).

5. According to published research by the APA, The Mayo Clinic, and Johns Hopkins Medicine.

6. Henry Cloud, *Integrity: The Courage to Meet the Demands of Reality* (New York: HarperCollins, 2006).

7. Jamil Zaki, "What, Me Care? Young Are Less Empathetic." *Scientific American* (January 2011).

8. Bill Strom, *More than Talk: Communication Studies and the Christian Faith* (Dubuque, IA: Kendall Hunt, 2013).

9. Patricia Ann Castelli, "An Integrated Model for Practicing Reflective Learning." *Academy of Educational Leadership Journal* Vol. 15, No. S1 (November 2011).

10. Henry Cloud and John Townsend, *How to Have That Difficult Conversation You've Been Avoiding* (Grand Rapids: Zondervan, 2003).

11. World Vision blog, https://www.worldvision.org/blog/social-justice-really-mean

12. Mary Poplin, *Finding Calcutta: What Mother Teresa Taught Me About Meaningful Work and Service* (Downers Grove, IL: Intervarsity Press, 2008).

13. James W. Sire, *The Universe Next Door* (Downers Grove, IL: InterVarsity Press, 4th Edition, 2004), 17.

14. Steve Wilkens and Mark Sanford, *Hidden Worldviews: Eight Cultural Stories that Shape Our Lives* (Downers Grove, IL: Intervarsity Press, 2009).

15. Roger Kimball, "Derrida and the Meaninglessness of Meaning." *Wall Street Journal,* Oct. 12, 2004.

16. Martin Luther, "Preface to his translation of St. Paul's Epistle to the Romans (1522)." *International Thesaurus of Quotations* (New York: HarperCollins, 1996), 214.

17. Tenth General Convention of the American Lutheran Church.

18. Stanley Grenz, "Theological Foundations for Male-Female Relationships." *Journal of the Evangelical Theological Society (JETS)* 41/4 (December 1998), 615-630.

19. Peter Kreeft, *Back to Virtue* (San Francisco: Ignatius Press, 1986), 156.

20. C.S. Lewis, *The Weight of Glory* (San Francisco: HarperOne, 2001), 45-46.

21. John Jefferson Davis, *Handbook of Basic Bible Texts* (Grand Rapids: Zondervan,1984).

22. John Townsend, *Leading From Your Gut: How You Can Succeed From Harnessing the Power of Your Values, Feelings, and Intuition* (Grand Rapids: Zondervan, 2018).

23. Gordon MacDonald, *Ordering Your Private World* (Nashville, Thomas Nelson, 1984), 176.

24. Frederick Buechner, *Wishful Thinking: A Seeker's ABC* (San Francisco: Harper One, 1993), 118-119.

25. Ibid.

ABOUT LOVE AND TRANSFORMATION INSTITUTE

LTI is a collective of forward-thinking leaders, educators, and innovators who have come together in order to create cultural change through leading research, experiential learning, digital technology, and media.

We are a collaborative organization dedicated to exploring innovative ways to transform individuals, families, organizations, and societies by changing how people on a global scale understand, experience, and integrate love into their lives, their relationships, and their communities.

At LTI we believe that love is the ultimate agent for transforming how people live and how organizations work. Love is more than a feeling. We believe love is a catalyst that, when applied to relationships, heals and transforms them. Toward this end, we develop resources and provide experiences that help people and teams put love into practice so that they can get healthy and grow.

For more information, visit LoveandTransformation.org

Assessments
Coaching
Consulting
Leadership Training
Organizational Development
Speaking
Symposiums
Workshops/Events

Ben Bost is the co-founder of Love and Transformation Institute. Ben is an innovator and executive mentor who provides resources to individuals and organizations as a catalyst for the transformational nature of love in culture.

Kent DelHousaye is the co-founder of Love and Transformation Institute. Kent is an executive coach, leadership consultant, and teaching pastor, working to help individuals and organizations get healthy and grow.